by Mark Stewart

ACKNOWLEDGMENTS

The editors wish to thank Cecil Fielder for his cooperation in preparing this book. Thanks also to Integrated Sports International for their assistance.

PHOTO CREDITS

All photos courtesy AP/Wide World Photos, Inc. except the following:

Louis Raynor/Sports Chrome – Cover, 30
Jeff Carlick/Sports Chrome – 9, 12, 43 top, 47 right
Sports Chrome – 6
Detroit Tigers – 6, 9
Mark Stewart – 48

STAFF

Project Coordinator: John Sammis, Cronopio Publishing
Series Design Concept: The Sloan Group
Design and Electronic Page Makeup: Jaffe Enterprises, and
    Digital Communications Services, Inc.

LIBRARY OF CONGRESS CATALOGING-IN-PUBLICATION DATA

Stewart, Mark.
    Cecil Fielder / by Mark Stewart.
        p. cm. – [Grolier all-pro biographies]
    Includes index.
    Summary: A brief biography of the Detroit Tigers first baseman.
    ISBN 0-516-20163-8 [lib. bdg.] — 0-516-26012-X [pbk.]
    1. 2. Baseball players—United States—Biography—Juvenile literature. 3. Detroit Tigers [Baseball team]—Juvenile literature. [1. Fielder, Cecil, 1963-   . 2. Baseball players.
    3. Afro-Americans—Biography.]
    I. Title. II. Series.
    GV865.F4266S84 1996
    796.357'092—dc20
    [B]   96-15144
                                                                                                    CIP
                                                                                                    AC

Grolier **ALL-PRO** Biographies™

Cecil

Fielder

by
Mark Stewart

CHILDREN'S PRESS®
A Division of Grolier Publishing
New York • London • Hong Kong • Sydney
Danbury, Connecticut

Contents

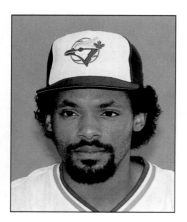

Who

Am I?

Everybody gets tested in life. The key to success is having the wisdom to make the right choice and the courage to stand behind it. I left this country when no one here would give me a chance to prove myself. It took a lot of courage, but it turned out to be the best choice I ever made. My name is Cecil Fielder, and this is my story . . . "

"Everybody gets tested in life."

Growing Up

From the first time Cecil Fielder squeezed into a Little League uniform, it was clear to everyone in the town of La Puente, California, that he was not at all like other children. Cecil was a big boy who did things in a big way. In fact, he pitched so well that a group of parents went to league officials and demanded that he be moved into a higher age group. Cecil, they claimed, was too large and too good to be playing against their ten- and eleven-year-olds. And Cecil was only eight!

No one doubted where Cecil's athletic ability came from—his parents. Cecil's father, Edson, had been an All-State shortstop in high school. His mother, Tina, had been a track star. Both parents worked very hard to support their three children. Edson Fielder was a janitor, and Tina worked at a variety of odd jobs to make ends meet.

Cecil's parents were proud of his athletic accomplishments, and they encouraged him to play sports. But no matter how many batters he struck out or how many baskets he made, Cecil

"Big things in big ways" can describe the life of Cecil Fielder.

was also expected to do his chores and help around the house. One of those chores was cooking dinner when his mother had to stay late at work. She would call Cecil and tell him exactly what to do, and he would follow her instructions perfectly.

When Cecil Fielder first started going to school, he took to some subjects right away, especially math. But what Cecil liked most of all was playing sports. He could have played them all the time.

That was not what his mother wanted to hear. She explained to Cecil that no matter how good an athlete he was, he needed to learn how to read, write, and just plain *think*. And his education would never happen on a baseball diamond or a basketball court. The rule in the Fielder house was "do your schoolwork and then you can play."

"It's really important to learn how to read well," says Cecil. "In our society today, you're just not going to make it without strong reading ability. If you're having trouble, you have to do what I did—commit yourself to working hard, don't be intimidated, and don't stop until you are the best you can be. To this day, I keep my eyes and ears open all the time, because I learned that education never really stops . . . unless you let it."

Throughout Cecil's childhood, he was an unstoppable force on the baseball field. During his Little League days, he once struck out 17 kids in a game. Years later, in high school, some opposing players thought he was a college player pretending to be 16!

From his parents and teachers, Cecil learned the importance of discipline. He saw how easy it was to improve if he applied himself and concentrated. This approach worked for the subjects he found difficult, such as English, and also in the sports he played. By the time Cecil enrolled at Nogales High

Mark Salas, Cecil's friend from childhood, made the major leagues as a catcher.

School, he was a well-rounded student, and one of the most popular kids in his class.

"I faced the same challenges most kids have to deal with when they grow up in a city. The peer pressure—that pressure to go along with everybody else—could be pretty powerful sometimes. When it came to drugs and alcohol, however, the choice was simple. I just said no."

Cecil was also the best athlete in town. He was a muscular 6' 3", with lightning-quick reflexes and amazing leaping ability. Cecil was an excellent football player. He was primarily a

Not considered a top prospect, Cecil became
the highest-paid player in baseball.

defensive back, but because of his strong arm, the coach often brought him in to throw long bombs to wide receiver Mark Salas. Mark later became a fine major-league catcher, and he and Cecil became teammates again on the Detroit Tigers! Cecil was also the star of the basketball team. He was impossible to guard, because he could swish a long jump shot or barrel down the lane for a rim-rattling dunk.

Although he was certain his future lay in basketball, Cecil decided to try out for the baseball team in the spring of his junior year. No one was surprised when he became the best player on that team, too. In fact, he earned All-State honors in each of the three sports he played.

Cecil was disappointed when he was not offered a basketball scholarship by a major university. He felt a little better when he learned that he had been drafted by the Baltimore Orioles, but he soon realized that they did not consider him a top prospect. His best offer was from the University of Nevada–Las Vegas (UNLV). The school had a great hoops program, but UNLV wanted him for its baseball team. Cecil accepted the offer and took his first step on the long road to baseball stardom.

Road to

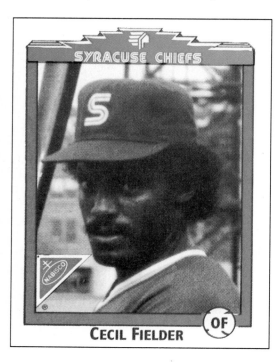

SYRACUSE CHIEFS

CECIL FIELDER — OF

Cecil Fielder played just a couple of games for UNLV, but in the year since leaving high school he had developed enough as a hitter to attract serious interest from several major-league teams. This time he was drafted by the Kansas City Royals, and they sent him to their minor-league team, the Syracuse Chiefs. There, he clubbed 20 home runs, 28 doubles, and knocked in 68 runs. Scouts for the Toronto Blue Jays were impressed and Toronto made a trade to acquire the young slugger. By July 1985, Cecil was in the major leagues, making big contributions to Toronto's pennant drive. He hit .311 and belted four homers in limited action.

the Pros

Willie Upshaw (right) was Toronto's starting first baseman until 1988. Fred McGriff (below) took over at first base for Toronto in 1988, keeping Cecil on the bench.

For the next two seasons, Cecil was the second-string first baseman behind Willie Upshaw. Yet when Upshaw left the team in 1988, it was not Cecil who replaced him, but another young power hitter, Fred McGriff. Because the team had veteran George Bell as its everyday designated hitter, Cecil found himself stuck on the bench.

At season's end, no major-league team was willing to give Cecil a starting job. When an offer came from the Hanshin Tigers in Japan, he realized this might be a great opportunity to showcase his talents. Cecil said goodbye to his Toronto teammates and prepared to play the 1989 season halfway around the world.

Cecil knew that he was taking a huge gamble. Many other American players had gone to Japan and failed because they could not cope with living so far from home. Cecil decided the best way to feel at home was to bring his family with him, and to try to learn as much about Japanese culture and customs as he could.

Cecil became a national sensation in Japan. His enormous size and his brilliant smile captivated fans, while his awesome home runs became the talk of Japanese baseball. In 106 games, Cecil hit 38 home runs and batted .302.

Cecil gave Japanese crowds a thrill with his hefty cuts at the plate, even when he swung and missed. They nick-named him *Ogata Senpuki*, or The Big Electric Fan.

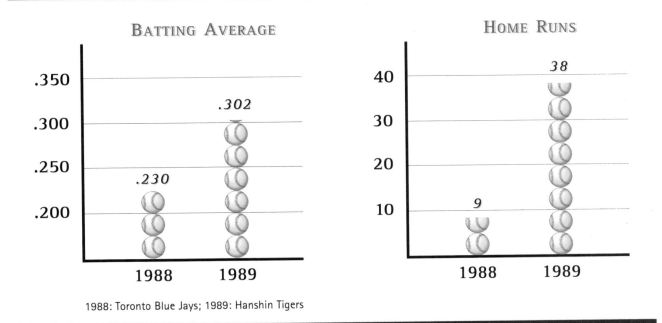

Cecil's 1989 Japanese baseball stats reveal his big improvement at the plate:

BATTING AVERAGE

.350
.300 — .302
.250
.230
.200

1988   1989

HOME RUNS

40 — 38
30
20
10 — 9

1988   1989

1988: Toronto Blue Jays; 1989: Hanshin Tigers

News of Cecil's exploits began to trickle back to the United States, where the Detroit Tigers—world champions just five years earlier—were losing 103 games.

After the Japanese baseball season ended, the Detroit Tigers offered Cecil a chance to return to the majors as their starting first baseman. He packed his bags for Detroit and prepared to start his "second" major-league career. Reflecting on his stint in Japan, Cecil says, "It was a good time for me and my family. Baseball is baseball—it was no different as far as playing the game."

The Story

When Detroit Tiger fans heard that Cecil Fielder would be their first baseman in 1990, they were not sure what to think. What kind of a player would he be in a big-league starting role? Cecil answered that question with his bat. He hammered 51 home runs in 1990, more than any American Leaguer had produced in 29 years. Cecil also led the majors with 132 RBIs. He did what he knew he could do all along. All he had ever needed was the chance to do it.

Cecil became one of the most popular players in baseball, and his power surge improved Detroit's record by 20 wins. In 1991, he proved

Cecil powers a grand slam home run.

he was for real by hitting 44 home runs and knocking in 133 runs. The Tigers continued to improve, rising to second place in the AL Eastern Division. And in 1992, Cecil tied the great Babe Ruth's record by leading the major leagues in RBIs for the third season in a row.

From 1990 to 1992, Cecil's RBI numbers were comparable to Babe Ruth's (bottom). Cecil's huge home runs made him the most popular player on the Tigers (top).

Since his return from Japan, Cecil has maintained a level of consistency that other players can only dream about. He bats around .260 almost every year, and is right up there with the league leaders in home runs and RBIs. He pounds left-handed pitching, holds his own against righties, and he can hit the ball out of any part of the park.

Cecil frightens pitchers because he hits the ball when it is thrown at his knees—right where pitchers are taught to pitch. In other words, what might be a brilliant pitch to another batter can be a disaster when Cecil is at the plate!

Do opposing hurlers hate Cecil? Not at all. They fear and respect him. And they appreciate that when he does slam a mammoth home run, he will not show up a pitcher by standing in the batter's box to watch the ball go over the wall.

Cecil blasts a low fastball.

Cecil is one of baseball's most beloved players, one of its greatest stories, and one of its most exciting hitters. There are only a handful of men in the majors whom fans will pay to see at the plate. And Cecil is definitely one of them.

"I know I'm not the best looking human being in the world. But I'm getting my job done. The game of baseball is not about looking good in the hotel lobby—if you don't perform, they'll run you out no matter what you look like!"

Timeline

1985: Makes major-league debut for Toronto Blue Jays

1990: Returns to the United States and hits 51 homers for the Detroit Tigers

1988: Plays last game for Toronto Blue Jays; signs contract with Hanshin Tigers of the Japanese Central League

1993: Becomes only the fifth Tiger ever to record four consecutive 100-RBI seasons

1992: Leads the major leagues in RBIs for the third straight year

1995: Hits his 250th major-league homer

Game

Action!

ecil went into the final game of the 1990 season with 49 home runs. He lined two balls into the left-field seats against the Yankees to finish with 51 round-trippers.

ecil hit his 100th and last minor-league home run for the Syracuse Chiefs in 1986.

ecil takes a positive approach to his work. "I basically want to get along with everybody, come to the ballpark, and be able to smile every day."

Cecil's favorite player is Kirby Puckett. Like Cecil, Kirby plays hard and has fun every time he wears a baseball uniform.

Cecil's hands are among the softest and quickest in the league. His mother thinks he developed this quality by taking three years of karate classes when he was a kid.

Legend Willie McCovey presents Cecil with a tape measure in honor of a mammoth home run Cecil hit in July 1993.

Cecil is the only player ever to hit a ball over the bleachers in Milwaukee's County Stadium, and he was the third to hit a ball completely over the roof at Tiger Stadium.

In 1990, Cecil hit three homers in a game on May 6, then did it again on June 6!

You know by the swing when it's gone—it's like you didn't hit a thing."

27

Dealing

When a dispute between players and owners ended the 1994 season and prevented the World Series from being played, Cecil Fielder could have just taken a vacation and waited for things to get back to normal. Instead, he took a leading role in the negotiations, flying all over the country to attend union meetings and bargaining sessions. Cecil made sure he was prepared by reading books about labor negotiations and collective bargaining.

"After what happened in the playoffs and World Series, I thought I should get involved. It woke me up and made me realize that there is more to this than what we do on the field."

Cecil faces reporters during baseball's labor dispute in 1994.

With It

Cecil and union chief Donald Fehr answer questions about the strike.

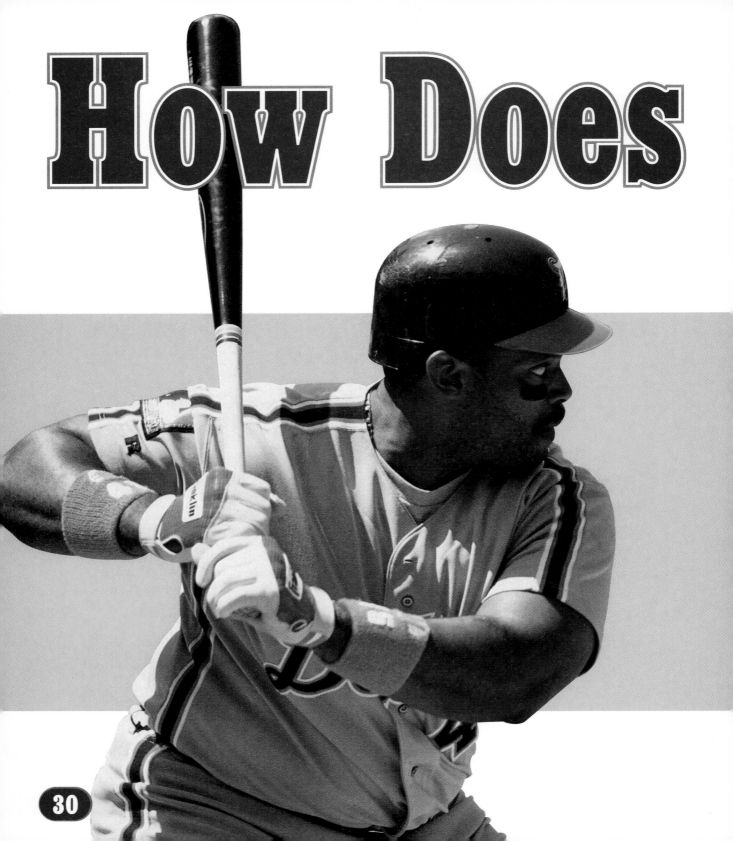

How Does

He Do It?

A key moment in Cecil Fielder's career came when he began working with Blue Jays hitting coach Cito Gaston after being called up from the minors. Cito told the young slugger that he needed to develop a "trigger"—some movement that he could repeat before each pitch, so he could cock his bat at just the right moment. Gaston now says he taught Cecil too well. That is because Gaston manages the Blue Jays, and has watched Cecil beat Toronto too many times.

"He taught me to rock to get me started, then to keep my hands back and swing."

The Grind

Taking it to the major leagues is easy compared to what a player must do to stay there. Opponents are always looking for a weakness or a flaw in your game. And when they find one, they will exploit it until you find a way to fight back. Cecil Fielder is constantly having to adjust to new pitching strategies, as pitchers keep trying to fool him at the plate.

"I think the hardest thing about being a professional athlete is remembering that you must keep on pushing at all times. Just because you made it to the top doesn't mean you're going to stay there without hard work."

Cecil takes working out and training seriously, but he always tries to have fun.

Family

During his senior year in high school, Cecil caught the eye of a girl named Stacey. She thought he was cute—until he stood up! She could not believe how big Cecil was, and how strangely he dressed, with his burnt-orange bell-bottoms and high-top basketball shoes. Stacey got over the initial shock of seeing Cecil. They started dating in high school and eventually got married. Cecil and Stacey Fielder have two children, Prince and Ceclyn. Ceclyn takes after her mother, while Prince takes after his father. Prince is the biggest kid on his baseball team, and a Little League All-Star.

"And he can hit!" says a very proud Cecil Fielder.

Matters

Cecil and Stacey arrive in Tokyo for a series of games between
U. S. and Japanese All-Stars.

Say What?

What do baseball people say about Cecil Fielder?

"I've never seen anything like him in all the years I've been in baseball."

—*Vada Pinson, former Detroit Tigers hitting instructor*

"He's unbelievably strong. It's hard to throw him a strike—he's on everything, you can't fool him."

—*Pat Borders, former Toronto teammate*

"He's capable of taking a ball that's down-and-away and hitting it out of the ballpark."

—*Chet Lemon, former Detroit Tigers outfielder*

"When I see the cigar in his mouth and the fur coat he has on sometimes—and the home runs he's hitting—I'm thinking I'm playing with another Babe Ruth!"

—*John Doherty, former Detroit teammate*

"Cecil is one of the few guys today that I really admire."

—*Willie McCovey, Hall of Famer*

Career

Cecil doubled against the Oakland A's in his first major-league at bat. He then collected hits in his next four games, beginning his career with a five-game hitting streak.

Cecil launches one on his way to winning the 1995 All-Star home run contest.

Cecil is the only man in Detroit Tigers history to hit 25 or more home runs in six consecutive seasons.

In 1990, Cecil led the majors in homers and RBIs, and he also topped the American League in total bases, extra-base hits, and slugging percentage.

Highlights

Cecil finished the 1995 season with 250 major-league home runs.

Cecil receives an RBI award from Hall of Famer Henry Aaron.

In 1991, Cecil led the major leagues in RBIs for a second consecutive season. The last American Leaguer to do that was Hall of Famer Jimmie Foxx, in 1932 and 1933. Cecil also became only the second Tiger to top 40 home runs in back-to-back seasons. Hall of Famer Hank Greenberg did it first, in 1937 and 1938.

Cecil gets a pat from Travis Fryman after a 1995 home run.

Reaching

Unlike many of today's athletes, Cecil Fielder understands the incredible injustices suffered by African-Americans in the early days of baseball. Until 1947, no African-Americans were allowed to play in the major leagues. Instead, they played in the Negro Leagues, where they made far less money than they might have in the majors. When the Tigers held a pre-game ceremony to celebrate the 75th anniversary of the Negro Leagues, Cecil bought all of the bleacher seats at Tiger Stadium and gave the tickets away for free.

"We were excited to honor the Negro Leagues, and I wanted to do something special for the fans."

Cecil loves the game of baseball and the fans love Cecil. Unlike some players, Cecil takes time to sign autographs whenever he can, no matter how long it takes.

Cecil and slugger Frank Thomas (seated second from right)
sign autographs for kids in a Japanese shopping mall.

Out

Cecil never charges
for his autograph,
and is always happy
to meet his fans.

Numbers

Name: Cecil Grant Fielder

Nickname: "Big Daddy"

Born: September 21, 1963

Height: 6' 3"

Weight: 260 pounds

Uniform Number: 45

College: University of Nevada–Las Vegas

Cecil holds an all-time record he probably does not want. He is the only player in history to play 1,000 games yet never steal a single base!

Year	Team	Games	Home Runs	RBIs	Batting Average	Slugging Average
1985	Toronto Blue Jays	30	4	16	.311	.527
1986	Toronto Blue Jays	34	4	13	.157	.325
1987	Toronto Blue Jays	82	14	32	.269	.560
1988	Toronto Blue Jays	74	9	23	.230	.431
1990	Detroit Tigers	159	51*	132*	.277	.592*
1991	Detroit Tigers	162*	44*	133*	.261	.513
1992	Detroit Tigers	155	35	124*	.244	.458
1993	Detroit Tigers	154	30	117	.267	.464
1994	Detroit Tigers	109	28	90	.259	.504
1995	Detroit Tigers	136	31	82	.243	.472
Totals		**1,095**	**250**	**762**	**.257**	**.497**

*Led American League

1989: Played in Japan

What If...

I've played ball my whole life, so I never thought much about what I might be doing if I hadn't made it as a major leaguer. I suppose I would have gone back to college, completed my education and found a career that interested me. I've always stood up for my convictions and believed in myself, and I have always loved to learn. I think that combination—along with hard work—would give me, or anyone else, a great chance to succeed outside of the baseball world."

Glossary

CONSECUTIVE several events that follow one after another

CONSISTENCY steady regularity

CONVICTIONS the moral principles and rules one believes in and lives by

COLLECTIVE BARGAINING negotiation between an employer and a labor union, usually concerning wages, hours, and working conditions

SHOWCASE to exhibit or show to others in an attractive manner

SURGE a sudden, extraordinary burst; spurt

THRIVE to grow and be successful

VETERAN one who has had a lot of experience

DISCIPLINE to teach good behavior, often using rewards and punishment

EXPLOIT to make productive use of an object or person

EXPLOITS notable acts or accomplishments

MASS bulk; size and weight

SCHOLARSHIP money given to a student to help pay for schooling

Index

About The Author

Mark Stewart grew up in New York City in the 1960s and 1970s—when the Mets, Jets, and Knicks all had championship teams. As a child, Mark read everything about sports he could lay his hands on. Today, he is one of the busiest sportswriters around. Since 1990, he has written close to 500 sports stories for kids, including profiles on more than 200 athletes, past and present. A graduate of Duke University, Mark served as senior editor of *Racquet*, a national tennis magazine, and was managing editor of *Super News*, a sporting goods industry newspaper. He is the author of every Grolier All-Pro Biography.